DATE DUE

BUILDING AMAZING STRUCTURES

Tunnels

NEW EDITION

Chris Oxlade

Heinemann Library
Chicago, Illinois

Revised and updated
© 2000, 2006 Heinemann Library
a division of Reed Elsevier Inc.
Chicago, Illinois

Customer Service 888-454-2279

Visit our website at www.heinemannraintree.com

Designed by Celia Floyd and Richard Parker (2nd edition)
Illustrations by Barry Atkinson
Originated by Modern Age
Printed and bound in China by WKT Company Ltd

10 09 08 07 06
10 9 8 7 6 5 4 3 2 1

Library of Congress Cataloging-in-Publication Data
Oxlade, Chris.
  Tunnels / Chris Oxlade.
     p. cm. -- (Building amazing structures)
  Includes bibliographical references and index.
  ISBN 1-4034-7906-2 (library binding-hardcover)
  1. Tunnels--Juvenile literature. 2. Tunneling--Juvenile literature. I. Title. II. Series.
  TA807.O95 2005
  624.1'93--dc22

                              2005024040

Acknowledgments
The publishers would like to thank the following for permission to reproduce photographs: Ann Ronan Picture Library pp. **7**, **26**, **29**; Associated Press p. **27** (Patrick Gardin); J. Allan Cash p. **8**; James Davis Travel Photography p. **11**; Massachusetts Turnpike Authority, USA p. **23**; QA Photos Ltd pp. **4**, **12**, **14**, **16**, **18**, **19**, **20**, **25**; Robert Harding p. **5**; Science Photo Library p. **21**; Taylor Woodrow p. **22**.

Cover photograph of the ventilation and escape tunnel on the Jubilee Line of the London Underground, United Kingdom reproduced with permission of constructionphotography.com (QA Photos/Jim Byrne).

Every effort has been made to contact copyright holders of any material reproduced in this book. Any omissions will be rectified in subsequent printings if notice is given to the publishers.

Contents

Some words are shown in bold, **like this**. You can find out what they mean by looking in the glossary.

About Tunnels

It is exciting to speed through a long, dark tunnel in a car or train. But have you ever wondered how this amazing underground passageway was made? Tunnels can go almost anywhere—under roads, railroad tracks or bustling city streets, even right through massive mountain ranges and deep under wide rivers!

Structure around a hole

A tunnel is a type of structure. A structure is an object built to resist a push or pull. A tunnel is a structure because it supports the thousands of tons of rock, earth or water above it, stopping them falling or flooding into the tunnel. This might seem confusing, because a tunnel is a hole! But it is the roof and sides of the tunnel that make up its structure. They also keep it waterproof.

Building a tunnel is a difficult job that can take several years. Tunnelers and their machinery work in dangerous conditions hundreds or thousands of feet underground. So why do we build tunnels and how are they built?

The Channel Tunnel runs under the sea between England and France. At 31.4 miles (50.5 kilometers) long, it is the second longest rail tunnel in the world. It took 8 years to build.

Why do we build tunnels?

You have probably travelled through many tunnels—on foot, in cars, buses and trains, and perhaps in boats. Transportion is one of the main reasons for building tunnels. A tunnel through a hill or mountain creates a shortcut. It saves traveling around a hill or climbing over a twisting, snowy mountain pass. A tunnel under a river or **strait** saves time traveling on a ferry. In city centers, tunnels allow trains to move efficiently under the busy streets.

Some tunnels carry water from **reservoirs** to towns and cities. Tunnels called penstocks are also built to carry water from reservoirs to **hydroelectric power** stations. Miners dig tunnels to reach deposits of **minerals** under the ground.

Railroad tunnels allow trains to travel at high speed through mountains or beneath roads.

FACTS ✛ It's a tunnel world record!

- Longest tunnel: Delaware Aqueduct, New York. Water supply tunnel. Completed: 1965. Length: 105 miles (169 kilometers).

- Deepest tunnel: Hitra Tunnel, Norway. Road tunnel. Completed: 1994. Depth: 866 feet (264 meters) below sea level.

- Biggest tunnel: Yerba Tunnel, San Francisco Bay, California. Road tunnel. Completed: 1936. Dimensions: 79 feet (24 meters) wide, 56 feet (17 meters) high.

Tunnels in the Past

Tens of thousands of years ago many people lived in caves. They probably made their caves larger by chipping away at the rocks, and might have joined caves together with tunnels. The first tunnels we know about were built by ancient civilizations, such as the Egyptians, about 4,000 years ago.

Tunnels in ancient times

Ancient people built tunnels for water supply. The tunnels were parts of **aqueducts**, structures that carried water from lakes and rivers to where it was needed for drinking and for **irrigating** crops. The tunnel builders had no machines or explosives. They broke the rock at the **tunnel face** with hammers and chisels. Another method they used was to heat the rock with fire to make it expand and then cool it quickly with water to make it crack.

In ancient times being a tunneler was a very nasty job. It was hot, dusty, and extremely dangerous. Most tunnelers were slaves, and hundreds or thousands were killed by rock falls during the building of each tunnel.

FACTS ✣ Amazing ancient tunnels

- The **Babylonians** built a pedestrian tunnel about half a mile (nearly 1 kilometer) long under the Euphrates River in modern-day Iraq, in about 2180 B.C.
- The Ancient Greeks drove a water-supply tunnel more than half a mile (nearly 1 kilometer) long and 6 feet (2 meters) across through limestone on the island of Samos.
- Starting in A.D. 41, Roman **engineers** built a tunnel 4 miles (6 kilometers) long to drain a lake. The job took 30,000 workers 10 years.

The Hoosac Tunnel in Massachusetts (1851–1875) was built using explosives and hand tools.

Tunnels for transport

In the 17th century, industry began to grow in Europe and canals became important for moving materials such as coal or timber. Tunnels were needed to take canals through hills. They were difficult to dig, but cheaper than building flights of **locks** to go over the hills. Dozens of canal tunnels were dug in Europe and North America, starting with one on the Canal du Midi in France, completed in 1692.

In the 19th century, more tunnels were needed as new railroad networks were built. By this time, high-power explosives and efficient **pneumatic** drills had made tunneling through rock much quicker than before. Tunnel builders began **blasting** their way through some of the world's great mountain ranges, such as the Alps in Europe and the Rockies in North America. Starting the 1820s, a new invention, called the **tunneling shield**, made it possible to dig safely through soft, waterlogged ground under rivers. The shield supported the ground, stopping it caving in as the tunnelers dug.

Types of Tunnel

Looking from the inside, all tunnels are really long, thin holes under the ground. The name that **engineers** give to a type of tunnel depends on the ground that it goes through and the method used to build it.

Going underground

Bedrock is solid rock which reaches many miles into the Earth. In hills and mountains, bedrock often appears at the surface, but in valleys there are normally thick layers of soft sand, mud, or clay on top of the bedrock, which tunnel engineers call soft ground. There is always some water in the ground, too. At a certain depth soft ground is completely **waterlogged**. Even solid rock has cracks in it called fissures that water runs through.

Rock tunnels are tunnels built through solid bedrock. These tunnels are normally found in hills and mountains. Soft-ground tunnels are tunnels built through soft, crumbly rocks or soft ground, such as mud or clay. **Subaqueous** tunnels are underwater tunnels built under rivers and **straits**.

This tunnel in Norway protects the railroad track and trains from being buried by avalanches.

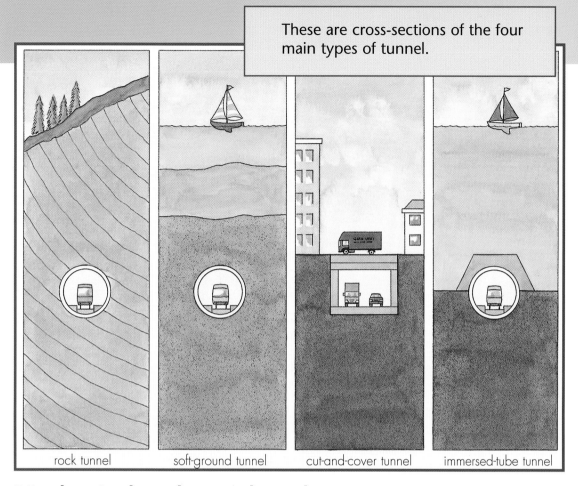

These are cross-sections of the four main types of tunnel.

| rock tunnel | soft-ground tunnel | cut-and-cover tunnel | immersed-tube tunnel |

Mechanical moles and explosives

There are four main ways of building a tunnel. In a rock tunnel, rock is removed by **blasting**. In soft rock or soft ground, a tunnel-boring machine called a **mole** cuts the tunnel. A cut-and-cover tunnel is made by digging a trench in the surface and covering it over with a roof. An immersed-tube tunnel is made by laying a tube along a river or sea bed.

Building a tunnel by blasting or with a mole is called driving a tunnel. Work takes place at the tunnel **heading**, where rock or soil—called **spoil**—is removed from the **tunnel face**, and carried backwards out of the tunnel. Supports are built to keep rock or soil from above falling into the freshly dug section of tunnel. A big mole can produce enough spoil to fill a wheelbarrow every two seconds. The Channel Tunnel moles dug out 10.4 million cubic yards (8 million cubic meters) of spoil—enough to fill nearly 100,000 train cars!

Shapes and Structures

The hole made by a tunnel is called a **bore**. Tunnels made up of just one bore are called single-bore tunnels. Tunnels with two bores are called twin-bore tunnels.

The bigger a tunnel's bore, the more difficult it is to build. The maximum size that is practical is about 33 feet (10 meters). It is often easier and quicker to build a twin-bore tunnel with small bores than a large single-bore tunnel. Twin-bore tunnels have passages connecting the two bores, and sometimes a small **service tunnel** lies between them.

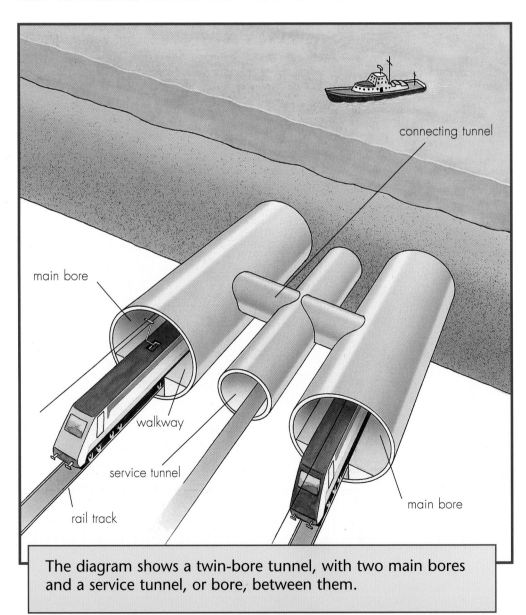

connecting tunnel

main bore

walkway

service tunnel

rail track

main bore

The diagram shows a twin-bore tunnel, with two main bores and a service tunnel, or bore, between them.

Special shapes

If you look at the **portal** of a long road or railway tunnel, you normally see a horseshoe shape. Tunnel bores that go deep underground have an arched roof like this because an arch is a very strong shape. It carries the massive weight of the rock and soil above the tunnel down around the sides and into the ground below.

This road tunnel in Switzerland shows the typical strong, arched shape of a tunnel bore.

Supports for safety

Rock and soil can fall from the roof and walls of an unsupported tunnel, which is dangerous for the tunnelers and delays tunneling. If the ground is soft, it can slump down, causing **subsidence** at ground level, which can damage the foundations of any buildings above the tunnel. The tunnel roof and walls, then, normally need to be supported with a tunnel **lining**. The lining holds any loose rock or soil in place, stops the ground above the tunnel from sagging, and stops water from leaking into the tunnel from the ground.

TRY THIS

Tunnel shapes

Cut two pieces of card, each 4 inches (10 centimeters) square. Fold one into a square-shaped tube and curl the other into a circular tube. Lay the tubes in the bottom of an old tray or shoe box. Carefully cover the centre of the tubes with sand or soil. Which tube keeps its shape best? Would it be best for a tunnel?

Tunnel Materials

A tunnel will only be strong and watertight if **engineers** choose the correct materials. The most important for building modern tunnels are concrete and steel. These are two truly amazing materials.

Uncrushable concrete

Concrete is the most widely used construction material. The ingredients of concrete are **cement**, water and aggregate, which is made up of sand and gravel. When the ingredients are first mixed, the concrete is runny. The cement and water react together and then harden to make a solid that holds the aggregate together. Normal concrete takes several hours to harden and about a month to reach its maximum strength.

Concrete is a good construction material because it is quite cheap and immensely strong. In fact, a mug-sized piece of concrete could support a 30-ton truck. It can easily be shaped by pouring it into moulds before it sets.

Shotcrete is special concrete that can be sprayed onto tunnel walls, where it sticks and sets.

Tunneling machinery is lifted by a crane so it can be lowered down a huge **shaft** to the tunnel **heading**.

Super-strong steel

Steel is an **alloy** made mostly of iron. Steel is used to make tunnel **linings** and temporary supports for tunnel walls and roofs. Steel must be protected from water to keep it from **rusting**. This is done by applying a waterproof layer of plastic or by **galvanizing** the steel.

Concrete is only strong when you try to squash it. If stretched, it cracks quite easily. However, steel is very strong when it is stretched. For example, a steel cable as thick as your finger could support a 30-ton truck. So where part of a structure made from concrete will be stretched, steel is added. This new material, made up of concrete and steel bars, is called reinforced concrete.

Double-quick setting

In the future, tunnel linings may be built with a completely new type of concrete, made with **resins** or **polymers** instead of cement. The new concrete would be more expensive, but it would set within a few minutes, allowing tunnelers to dig more quickly.

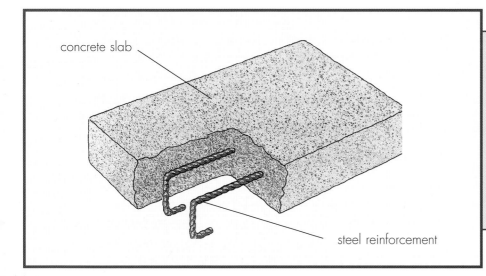

concrete slab

steel reinforcement

This simple reinforced concrete slab might be used in the roof of a cut-and-cover tunnel.

Designing a Tunnel

An organization decides that it needs to build a tunnel. For example, a railroad company wants to construct a tunnel to reduce journey times for its trains. But before the actual construction of the tunnel begins, much time will be spent on planning and designing it, with many experts brought in to help at every stage of the project. The first decision to make is how many **bores** the new tunnel needs, and how big the bores should be.

This diagram clearly shows how the Channel Tunnel links the United Kingdom and France.

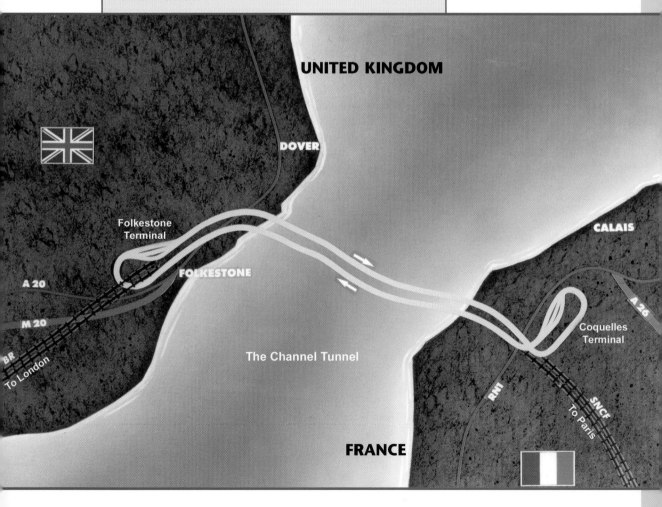

UNITED KINGDOM

DOVER

Folkestone
Terminal

FOLKESTONE

A 20

M 20

BR
To London

The Channel Tunnel

CALAIS

A 26

Coquelles
Terminal

RN1

SNCF
To Paris

FRANCE

Which way?

The easier it is to build a new tunnel, the cheaper it will be. This means avoiding rocks and soil that will be difficult and costly to tunnel through. So a **geological survey** of the ground on the planned route is carried out by a specialist **engineer**. The route of a tunnel must also avoid the foundations of buildings and other underground services, such as sewers and gas mains.

During this geological **investigation**, **boreholes** are dug and samples of the rocks and soils are tested to see how strong they are. The amount of water in the ground is also measured. The route of the tunnel might be changed if weak rock or lots of water are found.

After the investigation the details of the tunnel are worked out and drawings are made. The designer gives the tunnel builder all the information needed to build the tunnel, such as the tunnel's route, its size, and the materials to use.

New uses for tunnels

Transportation tunnels create a clear path for vehicles and trains. They also help to reduce environmental problems, such as noise and exhaust fumes. In the future, as tunneling techniques improve, new roads and railroads might run through rock tunnels deep underground. Cities could be linked by high-speed underground transit systems, with vehicles travelling at more than 300 miles (500 kilometers) per hour.

Site Preparation

Building a long road or railway tunnel is an enormous construction project that can take several years. Normally one **engineering** company, called the main contractor, organizes the whole construction job. There are also dozens of smaller companies called sub-contractors, who do special jobs such as **blasting**, **surveying**, or supplying concrete. Before construction of the tunnel itself can start, the construction site must be made ready.

Digging from both ends

Tunnels are normally dug from both ends at once. Where possible, **shafts** are dug down from the surface so that **spoil** can be removed up through them instead of back along the tunnel itself.

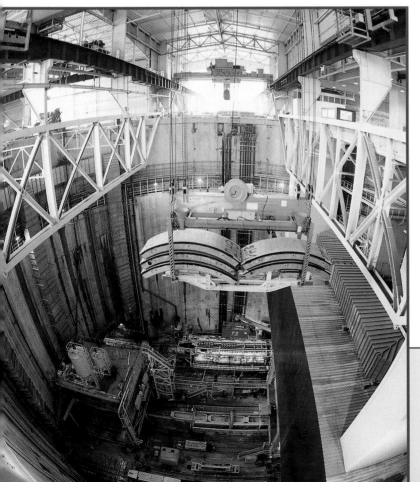

Digging sometimes starts in the middle of the tunnel, too. Machinery and materials are lowered down a huge shaft. At the French end of the Channel Tunnel, a shaft 180 feet (55 meters) across and 250 feet (75 meters) deep was dug.

Sections of tunnel **lining** are lowered into the Channel Tunnel for transport by train to the tunnel heading.

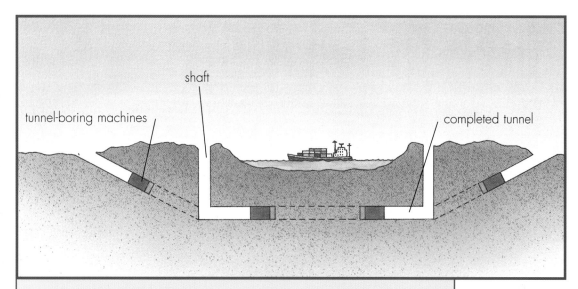

shaft

tunnel-boring machines

completed tunnel

This shows how four tunnel-boring machines can be used to dig an underwater tunnel.

Fighting floods

Water is a big problem for tunnel builders. It can flow in as a tunnel is dug, carrying sand or mud with it. In some tunnels there have been inflows of more than 66,000 gallons (250,000 liters)—enough to fill five bathtubs every second. This is dangerous for workers, and sometimes buries machinery and stops the tunnelling. Engineers often drill **boreholes** from the surface along the line of the tunnel to lower the **water table**. They can also pump **grout** into the ground, which sets, filling gaps in the rock or soil that water could flow through.

FACTS ✧ Under pressure

One way of stopping water from flowing in is to pressurize the tunnel. An airtight seal is placed behind the tunnel **heading** and air is pumped into the heading. The increased **air pressure** tries to push water back into the rocks.

Boring in Soft Ground

In soft rocks, a tunnel-boring machine or **mole** bores through the rock. The **tunnel face**, roof and sides must be supported to keep them from collapsing as digging progresses. As the mole moves forwards, cutting at the tunnel face, a tunnel **lining** is added behind it. The tunnelers must always be prepared for the unexpected, such as ground containing water, or a layer of hard rock.

Mega moles

A mole is shaped like a cylinder. The cylinder has the same diameter as the tunnel **bore** it digs. At the front is a rotating circular cutting head, with hard metal teeth that scrape away the rock. The cutting head is pushed forwards by **hydraulic rams**. Behind the cutting head the cylinder supports the tunnel roof and sides. Machinery just behind the cylinder

lifts sections of lining into place. Moles for major tunnels are gigantic machines. The largest Channel Tunnel machine weighed 1,575 tons and was 29 feet (8.75 meters) across and twice the length of a football field!

Here, a section of tunnel lining is being placed. Spoil is being removed by the **conveyor**.

This is one of the massive Channel Tunnel tunnel-boring machines. The cutting head is on the left.

Moles on the move

As a mole cuts through the ground, **spoil** falls through holes in the cutting head. It is carried on a conveyor belt to trucks or train cars that carry it out of the tunnel. Modern moles can dig through rock such as chalk at up to 660 feet (200 meters) a day. That may not sound like much, but it would take a person about two months to do the same amount of digging!

The mole is steered to make the tunnel turn left or right and to move towards the surface or deeper underground. Some moles are steered automatically by a laser beam fired along the tunnel, which gives the mole a perfectly straight line to follow.

TRY THIS
Catastrophic collapses
Make a pile of sand or soil at least 4 inches (10 centimeters) high outdoors on a flat surface. Try digging a circular tunnel an inch or so (a few centimeters) wide through the sand. Use a small stick to dig away the sand. Can you see how the roof and walls collapse? The wider you try to make the tunnel, the worse the collapses become. The cylinder of a tunneling mole keeps this from happening.

Digging into Rock

Tunnels through hard rock are driven by **blasting** away the rock at the **heading** with explosives. Because the rock is solid, the roof and walls of the new tunnel support themselves. But the blasting often weakens the rock around the tunnel, so tunnel **lining** is normally added for strength and to stop loose pieces of rock falling into the tunnel.

Explosives are placed in drilled holes before being detonated by electricity—at a safe distance.

Blasting and mucking

The blasting process is a cycle that is repeated again and again when building a tunnel. The first stage is to drill several deep holes into the **tunnel face** using **pneumatic** drills. The drills are mounted on a vehicle called a jumbo. When the holes are deep enough, the jumbo is moved back down the tunnel and explosive charges are put in the holes. The workers move a safe distance away and the charges are detonated with electric **fuses**.

A **ventilation** system pumps dust and fumes created by the explosions out of the tunnel. A mechanical loader picks up the rubble and puts it on to a conveyor belt, which carries it to waiting trucks or train cars. Removing the rubble is called mucking. The jumbo is moved back into place and the cycle starts again. In hard rock, the tunnel can progrss at about 65 feet (20 meters) a day.

Drilling and blasting are also used to create vast underground chambers. This cathedral-sized turbine hall of a **hydroelectric power** station is 492 feet (150 meters) underground.

A smooth finish

Blasting leaves a jagged tunnel, often with loose pieces of rock. So as the heading moves forward, the tunnel roof and walls are supported with steel arches or **shotcrete**. Later a concrete lining is added. Steel or wooden moulds called formwork are placed around the roof and walls and concrete is pumped behind them. When the concrete is set, the formwork is removed, leaving a smooth lining. Steel roof supports are also used in mining tunnels, which may be dug by blasting or by hand-held drilling machines.

In hot water

Tunnels through mountains often go through **bedrock** thousands of feet below the mountaintops. In these deep tunnels, the rocks and any water in them can be hot, creating extra problems for tunnelers. For example, during the building of the Simplon railway tunnel, which travels more than 6,500 feet (2,000 meters) under the Alps between Italy and Switzerland, tunnelers had to cope with scalding hot water at 130 °F (54 °C) flowing into the workings.

Ready-made Tunnels

Tunnel builders think of driving tunnels underground with **moles** or explosives as true tunnelling, because the rock and soil above the tunnel stay in place. Two other types of tunnels, cut-and-cover tunnels and immersed-tube tunnels, are constructed from above ground instead.

Cutting and covering

The cut-and-cover tunnelling method is used to build tunnels near the surface, such as **pedestrian** subways. There are three stages in building a cut-and-cover tunnel. A trench is dug along the line of the tunnel, the tunnel **lining** is placed in the trench, and then soil is put back on top.

The tunnel lining normally comes in **precast** sections of **reinforced concrete**, which are lowered into the trench and joined together. Using precast sections speeds up building, which is important because cut-and-cover tunnels are often built in very busy streets.

The reinforced concrete roof of this cut-and-cover tunnel is now complete.

Sinking sections

The immersed tube is the newest tunneling method. It was first used in 1906 for a railroad tunnel under the Detroit River. The tunnel is made up of sections of tube joined together to make a long tube that lies on a river bottom or seabed. The tube resists the huge pressure of water outside. In a river 165 feet (50 meters) deep, the pressure is the same as a huge truck resting on every square yard of the tunnel. Think of that next time you go through a tunnel under a river!

The first step in building an immersed-tube tunnel is to place **prefabricated** sections of tube in a trench in the riverbed, join them together, and weigh them down with tons of concrete. The tube is then covered over with concrete or gravel to protect it.

A section of twin-bore immersed-tube tunnel is moved into position by tugs.

TRY THIS

Pushing a pipe

Another method of tunnelling through soft ground, which is used for small-bore water tunnels, is called pipe-jacking. In pipe-jacking, the tunnel lining itself does the digging. Try this experiment to see how it works. Make a tube, about 4 inches (10 centimeters) long and 2 inches (5 centimeters) across, from card. Push it slowly into a pile of damp sand. After an inch or two (a few centimeters), pull the sand inside the tube out with a small stick. Now push the tube forward again.

Tunnels in Use

After construction work on a tunnel is completed, the tunnel is prepared for use. All the construction machinery, such as the **spoil**-removal trucks and digging **moles**, is removed from the site. Sometimes it is easier to leave moles under the ground instead of taking them apart and removing them, especially if the moles have been specially built and would be no good for building another tunnel.

Adding services

In a transportation tunnel, the road surface or railroad track is laid through the tunnel. Services, such as lighting, electricity, communications, and water, are added along the whole length of the tunnel, as well as traffic control lights or railway signals. Emergency equipment, such as fire alarms and **sprinklers**, is placed at regular intervals along the tunnel. Watertight doors, which seal off sections of a tunnel if water floods in, and fireproof doors, are put in place.

Ventilation is also very important. Engine exhaust fumes have to be removed and fresh air supplied for people to breathe. This is done with electric fans and air ducts.

Fresh air first

The first long road tunnel in the world was the Holland Tunnel under the Hudson River in New York, completed in 1927. Its designer, Clifford Holland, had to solve the problem of exhaust fumes from the cars in the tunnel. He did this by installing fans in the tunnel roof and a duct under the roadway. The fans suck polluted air out of the tunnel, which is replaced by fresh air from the duct.

In an emergency...

The biggest danger in transportion tunnels is fire. If a fire starts in a vehicle or train, the tunnel becomes blocked. Heat from the fire cannot escape upwards and the temperature gets very high. Smoke and fumes also spread quickly along the tunnel. So it is important for tunnel operators and the emergency services to have emergency procedures to evacuate tunnels safely and quickly. These procedures have to be practised regularly so that everybody in the emergency team knows what to do.

These fire crews are practicing what they would do in the event of an emergency.

Tunnel Disasters

Things can always go wrong as a tunnel is built. The tunnel roof or walls can collapse, water can flood in, or unexpected types of rock may be encountered. Accidents can also happen once a tunnel is completed and in use.

Building problems

- LÖTSCHBERG TUNNEL In 1908, water and gravel poured into a **heading** on the Lötschberg Tunnel under the Swiss Alps. More than half a mile (1 kilometer) of tunnel was filled with debris and 25 tunnellers were killed. They had thought they were digging into **bedrock**, but they had hit soft ground under a river valley.

- TANNA TUNNEL The Tanna Tunnel, a rock tunnel built in the 1920s in Japan, suffered many problems. One surge of water killed sixteen workers and trapped fifteen others, who were dug out seven days later.

- LONDON UNDERGROUND In July 2005, three terrorist bombs exploded on trains traveling though London underground train tunnels, killing thirty-nine passengers.

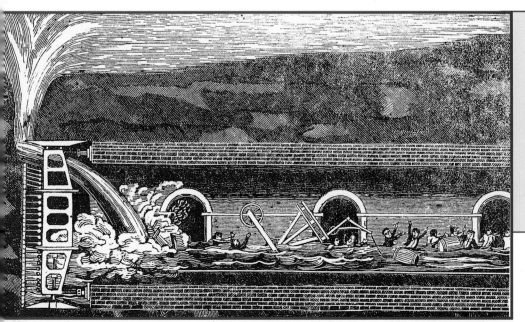

Water gushes into the heading of the Thames Tunnel, London, in 1828, killing six tunnelers.

SEIKAN TUNNEL Builders of the world's longest underwater tunnel, the 33.5-mile (54-kilometer) Seikan Tunnel in Japan, encountered very difficult rock conditions. The tunnel took twice as long to build and cost ten times as much as was planned. Sixty-six workers were killed in accidents.

Problems in use

- MONT BLANC TUNNEL In March 1999, a truck carrying flour and margarine caught fire in the Mont Blanc Tunnel, between Italy and France. Dozens of vehicles came to a stop in the tunnel. At least 39 people died in the fire and from inhaling smoke and fumes. Because of the intense heat it took two days to put the fire out. It is thought that extra air pumped into the tunnel to help people breathe made the fire burn more fiercely.

Shown here are the remains of a fire truck destroyed in the Mont Blanc Tunnel fire in 1999.

- HOLLAND TUNNEL In 1949, a truck carrying flammable chemicals caught fire and exploded in the Holland Tunnel, New York. About 500 feet (150 meters) of the tunnel was damaged, and many vehicles were destroyed. But thanks to the **ventilation** system, nobody was killed.

27

Tunnel Facts

The world's longest road tunnels

TUNNEL (YEAR COMPLETED)	LENGTH (MI.)	(KM)
Laerdal, Norway (2000)	15.0	24.5
St Gotthard, Switzerland (1980)	10.5	16.9
Arlberg, Austria (1978)	8.7	14.0
Hsuehshan, Taiwan (2005)	8.0	12.9
Fréjus, France–Italy (1980)	8.0	12.9
Mont Blanc, France–Italy (1965)	7.2	11.6

The Laerdal Tunnel takes fifteen minutes to drive through!

The world's longest rail tunnels

TUNNEL (YEAR OPEN)	LENGTH (MI.)	(KM)
Seikan, Japan (1988)	33.5	53.9
Channel Tunnel, UK-France (1994)	31.4	50.5
Moscow Metro, Russia (1979)	19.1	30.7
London Underground, UK (1939)	17.3	27.9
Dai-shimizu, Japan (1982)	13.8	22.2
Simplon II, Switzerland (1922)	12.3	19.8

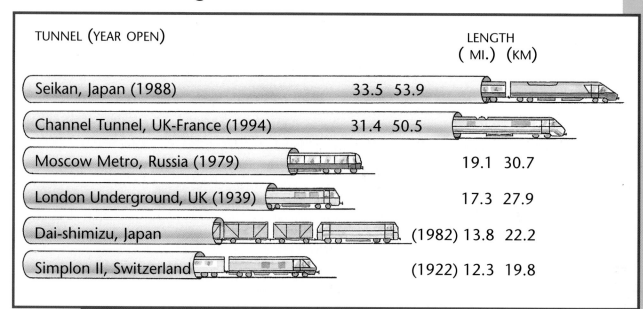

The Seikan Tunnel is also the world's longest underwater tunnel, although the Channel Tunnel has more of its length actually under water.

This is an 1851 design for a tunnel under the English Channel, designed to be built with iron tubes.

FACTS ✛ Tunneling firsts

- First canal tunnel and first use of explosives: Canal du Midi Tunnel, France. Completed: 1681. Length: 508 feet (155 meters).

- First underwater tunnel and first use of **tunneling shield**: Thames Tunnel, London, England. Completed: 1843. Original length: 1,200 feet (366 meters). Now part of London Underground system.

- The inventor of the tunneling shield, the **engineer** Marc Isambard Brunel, got the idea for his machine from watching a tiny **mollusk** called a teredo, or shipworm. Brunel watched it boring through wood in its shell, pushing sawdust out behind it.

- First rail tunnel: Mont Cenis, France–Italy. Completed: 1871. Length: 8.5 miles (13.7 kilometers).

- First use of high explosives and compressed air drills: Hoosac Tunnel, Massachusetts. Completed: 1875. Length: 4.7 miles (7.6 kilometers). It was the first to use **ventilation**.

- First road tunnel: Holland Tunnel, New York. Completed: 1927. Length: 1.6 miles (2.6 kilometers).

- First immersed-tube tunnel: Detroit River Railroad Tunnel, Ontario, Canada. Completed: 1906.

- First alpine road tunnel: Mont Blanc Tunnel, France–Italy. Completed: 1965. Length: 7.2 miles (11.6 kilometers).

Glossary

air pressure pressure of the air pushing against something

alloy material made of a metal combined with another metal or other substance

aqueduct channel that carries water. The channel may be made of pipes, tunnels and bridges.

Babylonia ancient empire that flourished in the second millennium B.C. in the area known today as the Middle East

bedrock hard, solid rock deep underground

blast break up rock using explosives

bore single hole through the ground

borehole deep, narrow hole bored down into the ground to take samples of the earth and rocks below

cement mixture of materials that hardens into a rock-like substance after it is mixed with water

conveyor belt or machine to move things on

engineer person who designs or builds structures

fuse short piece of wire used to make explosives ignite

galvanize cover steel with a coating of zinc to protect it from rusting

geological to do with the rocks that make up the Earth

grout mixture of cement and water. It is used to make earth or loose rock waterproof.

heading area near the tunnel face where tunneling work is being carried out

hydraulic ram machine with a piston and a cylinder filled with liquid. Pumping more liquid into the cylinder makes the piston move in or out.

hydroelectric power power, normally in the form of electricity, made by letting water flow through a turbine

investigate collect information about something

irrigate collect water and make it flow to where it is needed to water growing crops

lining covering on the inside of a tunnel that supports the ground around the tunnel and keeps water from flowing into it

lock a step on a canal that allows ships to move uphill and downhill

mineral chemical substance that is found in the ground

mole machine that bores through the ground

mollusk creature, such as a snail, with a soft body and a hard shell

pedestrian   person walking

pneumatic   powered by air

polymer   chemical with very long molecules. Rubber, silk and plastics are polymers.

portal   entrance to a tunnel

precast   set into a shape before it is put in place

prefabricated   made from parts built in a factory

reinforced concrete   concrete that has steel reinforcing bars embedded in it

reservoir   artificial lake that forms behind a dam

resin   yellow or brown transparent substance, sometimes very hard and sometimes soft and sticky. Sap from a fir tree is a resin.

rust   brown, flaky substance formed when iron reacts with air and water

service tunnel   small tunnel next to a larger tunnel that can be used to reach its different parts

shaft   hole leading from the ground to a tunnel below

shotcrete   thick liquid concrete sprayed onto a tunnel wall, where it hardens

spoil   rock or soil dug from a tunnel face

sprinkler   device that sprays water on to a fire

strait   narrow stretch of water that connects two larger bodies of water

subaqueous   underwater

subsidence   when the earth or rock underground collapses slightly, so that the surface sinks downwards

survey   to measure the ground so that something can be built on it

tunnel face   area of rock or ground at the very end of a tunnel that is dug away as the tunnel is built

tunneling shield   shield that keeps a soft tunnel face from collapsing as it is dug away

ventilation   circulation of fresh air

water table   the top of the layer of ground which is full of water

waterlogged   saturated with water

More Books to Read

Fine, Jil. *The Chunnel*. Danbury, Conn.: Children's Press, 2004.

Swanson, Diane. *Tunnels!* Toronto, Ontario, Canada: Annick Press, 2003.

Thomas, Mark. *The Seikan Railroad Tunnel*. New York: Rosen, 2001.

Index